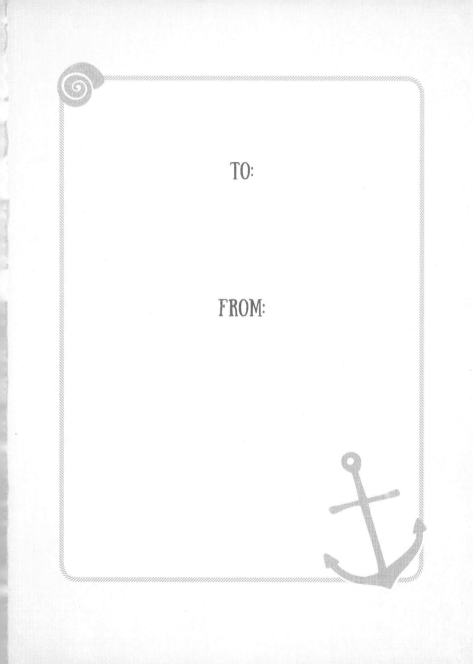

TO:

FROM:

LIFE IS BETTER at the BEACH

CHRISTINA VINSON

THOMAS NELSON
Since 1798

LIFE IS BETTER AT THE BEACH

© 2016 by Thomas Nelson

Published in Nashville, Tennessee, by Thomas Nelson. Thomas Nelson is a registered trademark of HarperCollins Christian Publishing, Inc.

Thomas Nelson titles may be purchased in bulk for educational, business, fund-raising, or sales promotional use. For information, please e-mail SpecialMarkets@ThomasNelson.com.

Unless otherwise noted, Scripture quotations are taken from the Holy Bible, New International Version®, NIV®. Copyright © 1973, 1978, 1984, 2011 by Biblica, Inc.® Used by permission of Zondervan. All rights reserved worldwide. www.zondervan.com. The "NIV" and "New International Version" are trademarks registered in the United States Patent and Trademark Office by Biblica, Inc.®

Scripture quotations marked CEB are taken from the Common English Bible. Copyright © 2011 Common English Bible.

Scripture quotations marked ESV are taken from the ESV® Bible (The Holy Bible, English Standard Version®). Copyright © 2001 by Crossway, a publishing ministry of Good News Publishers. Used by permission. All rights reserved.

Scripture quotations marked NASB are taken from New American Standard Bible®. Copyright © 1960, 1962, 1963, 1968, 1971, 1972, 1973, 1975, 1977, 1995 by The Lockman Foundation. Used by permission. (www.Lockman.org)

Scripture quotations marked NLT are taken from the Holy Bible, New Living Translation. © 1996, 2004, 2007, 2013 by Tyndale House Foundation. Used by permission of Tyndale House Publishers, Inc., Carol Stream, Illinois 60188. All rights reserved.

Scripture quotations marked TLB are taken from The Living Bible. Copyright © 1971. Used by permission of Tyndale House Publishers, Inc., Carol Stream, Illinois 60188. All rights reserved.

Scripture quotations marked MSG are from The Message by Eugene H. Peterson. © 1993, 1994, 1995, 1996, 2000. Used by permission of NavPress Publishing Group. All rights reserved.

ISBN-13: 978-0-7180-8968-9

Printed in China

16 17 18 19 20 DSC 6 5 4 3 2 1

 Contents

Beach Rule #1:

⚓ WAKE up SMILING.

Yawn. Stretch. You sit up and smile.

The sun is beginning to stream softly through the windows, and the sea breeze flutters the curtains. It's time to wake up.

Mornings at the beach are completely different from everyday mornings at home, aren't they? When you're on vacation, mornings have no sense of urgency. Alarm clocks aren't blaring, lunches don't need to be packed, and no appointments fill your agenda—unless you count slowly sipping coffee with your loved ones or teaching your little ones how to jump the waves.

Waking up at the beach means you wake up smiling because there's an entire day to be enjoyed, and it's beckoning you to dive right in.

You may wonder, *Is it possible to wake up smiling in my everyday, non-beach life?* Life at the beach seems so easy, while "real life" has so many more demands. Rest assured, it *is* possible to wake up smiling, regardless of your location. Whether you're waking up at an oceanfront estate or in the suburbs of Chicago, you have one great promise that can bring great joy: the Lord's mercies are new every morning.

God wipes your slate clean time and time again. With the sunrise each day, you have the blessed assurance that He loves you. He gives you a fresh start each day, for all the days of your life.

If you can remember that great promise when you wake up in the morning, your day will start off on a positive note. No, you can't forego your daily responsibilities. Kids still need to be carpooled, work still needs to be completed, and cars still need to be fixed. But with the morning comes a new beginning, a genesis. And that's enough reason to smile.

"BECAUSE OF THE LORD'S
GREAT LOVE WE ARE NOT CONSUMED,
FOR HIS COMPASSIONS NEVER FAIL.
THEY ARE NEW EVERY MORNING;
GREAT IS YOUR FAITHFULNESS."

—LAMENTATIONS 3:22–23

A grateful heart is a happy heart.

This old adage rings true even today. At the beach it's incredibly easy to cultivate a heart of gratitude. Your toes sink deep in the sugary sand, the sun shines bright overhead, and you take a nap on the screened-in porch. Even a lunch of peanut butter sandwiches tastes good after a day at the beach.

Being grateful comes easily when you're enjoying a relaxing vacation. The hard part is being grateful once the vacation ends.

After you clean the sand out of your sandals, your sunburn begins to peel, and everyday life resumes, it's easy to see the difficulties and annoyances. But reflect, for a moment, on how your life would change if you chose each day to have a grateful attitude.

Look around right now. Is your refrigerator fully stocked? Thank God for His provisions of groceries, the money that paid for your food, and even the transportation that took you to the grocery store. Can you hear the birds singing outside? Thank the Lord for His creation and that He cares for the lowly sparrow, and even more for you. Are you protected from the outdoor elements? Remind yourself to be grateful for your home and the safety it provides.

Once you begin to have eyes of gratitude, it will become a habit—one that tunes your heart to sing a new song.

Whether you're watching the sunrise while standing on the shore or driving to work, breathe out a prayer of gratitude. When your alarm goes off in the morning, let your heart rejoice in a day full of unexpected graces and gifts. When you sink into bed at night, reflect on how the Lord sustained you throughout the day. Be mindful of the blessings in each day, and your heart will be transformed. A grateful heart is a happy heart indeed.

"IN ORDINARY LIFE
WE HARDLY REALIZE
THAT WE RECEIVE A
GREAT DEAL MORE THAN
WE GIVE,
AND THAT IT IS ONLY
WITH GRATITUDE
THAT LIFE BECOMES RICH."

—DIETRICH BONHOEFFER

When you're vacationing at the beach,

do you wake up and think, *This is going to be a terrible day,* or *I am dreading all this sunny weather,* or *I wish this week would end already*? The answer is always a resounding *no.* Life at the beach is full of hopeful expectation. You begin the day with a cheer, a smile, and a happy heart, for there's so much fun in store.

Why can you live in hopeful expectation all the time? Because of God's goodness—His ability to place tiny and big blessings in your day. You can live in expectation because God tells you to hope, to not give in to despair, and to trust in Him. He wouldn't speak those words if He didn't have good things in store for you.

Just as you know you will find treasures on the beach and feel the unexpected cool breeze when the humidity peaks, you can expect, with a hopeful heart, that God will show His goodness to you. It may not be in the way you envisioned, and it might not happen right away, but He will always come through—and exceed your expectations.

"Refuse to
be average.
Let your heart soar
as high as it will."
—A. W. Tozer

Beach Rule #2:

SHOES *are* OPTIONAL.

13

At the beach you relax your standards.

You don't need to fuss with the hair dryer, a bathing suit and bare feet is the dress code, and the only must-have toiletry is sunscreen. Letting go of the need to appear put together is one of the best parts of being at the beach. It's freeing, isn't it?

Sand gets tracked in, and wet towels hang in strange places. Perfectionism just doesn't belong at the beach, and you happily leave it at the door.

However, the same can't always be said when you return to normal life. It's a common pattern: you let yourself relax at the beach, but once vacation's over, you feel the need to appear put together—in every area of your life. The shoes go back on; the makeup routine begins again, throw pillows are fluffed and rearranged. None of those things is inherently bad, but if you're doing them out of concern for how you and your life are perceived, maybe it's time to think back to your days at the beach.

Remember that carefree feeling you had? It's possible to transfer that barefoot mentality into everyday life. You just need to let go of perfectionism for a bit. Let the laundry sit for another hour while you relax with a cup of tea. Let your children jump in mud puddles without worrying about the mess. Let the pressures of today roll off your shoulders as you think back on fond memories at the beach, and walk around your house barefoot—just to remind yourself what it's like.

"The LORD does not look
at the things people look at.
People look at the outward
appearance, but the LORD
looks at the heart."

—1 Samuel 16:7

Sand invites you to kick off your shoes.

The beach beckons you to dig your toes down deep. Waves of water cool off your feet when the sun gets too warm.

When you're at home, the act of going barefoot is probably a common occurrence too. It feels good to put up your feet. Whether your toes are perfectly proportioned or a little uneven, manicured or not, it doesn't matter—when you're at home, the shoes come off. At home being comfortable is key.

When you have company over to your house, the same applies to them. You welcome guests at the door. "Come in," you say. "Take off your shoes and stay awhile." Your guests happily oblige and pad around your home in their socks or bare feet. You're allowing your friends to treat your home as if it were theirs.

Some days you and your guests may track in sand. Other days snow or sleet might follow you in. Regardless of the season, you can always make your home comfortable for you and for your guests.

"Welcome home," you say. "Take off your shoes."

A little *sand* between
your *toes* always takes
away your *woes*.

After a relaxing day by the water,

your feet are probably covered with tiny grains of sand. In order not to track a sandbox's worth of sand into your home (or worse, into your bed!), you rinse off your feet before walking inside.

The Bible talks about feet numerous times, and one of the best-known stories involves Jesus and the disciples. More specifically, Jesus washed His followers' feet, which in those times was an extreme posture of servanthood and humility. Jesus washed His disciples' feet free of grime and sand and the elements, and He did it because He loved them.

The thought of washing others' feet may make you feel uncomfortable, and it's not done often in today's culture, but you can still live with a servant's heart. It could be a big step, like volunteering at your church or the local mission, but being a servant can simply mean a change in your mind-set.

Instead of grumbling about the sink of dishes your spouse was supposed to wash, grab a sponge and clean them as a simple act of love. When your neighbor's loose trash flies into your yard, pick it up and throw it away without complaint. If you see someone in need of help, stop to lend a hand instead of thinking, *I don't have time*. Sometimes a loving act just means biting your tongue instead of blurting out a harsh retort.

When you serve others in humility, you're washing their feet. You're showing them Christ and His character.

"THE MEASURE OF A
LIFE, AFTER ALL, IS NOT ITS
DURATION, BUT ITS DONATION."
—CORRIE TEN BOOM

Beach Rule #3:

SOAK up the SUN.

Sunshine? Check. Sunblock? Check.

Lots of time to sit and soak in the sun? Check. The beach is a great place to sit back, relax, and just *be* while you're basking in the warmth of the sun's rays. Sometimes it's on a towel with full sun overhead. If you're sensitive to the sun, it's under an umbrella with plenty of SPF. But either way, you have time to sit and soak in the fresh air and the warm temperature.

It goes without saying that today's culture is fast and frenzied. Our to-do lists are never ending, and if we're sitting, it's usually in front of a computer while working. Now, more than ever before, we don't sit for pleasure—we're always on the move.

When you're sitting at the beach, you have time to think about life and to ruminate over your present choices or the next six months. There's space to take deep breaths and to enjoy the stunning scenery around you instead of watching the sunset from your car. You have margin to pray quietly and sit in the Lord's presence. But once you leave the beach, often that time goes out the window.

Take heart. You don't need to live that way. You *can* make time to sit in the quiet, just you and God. All it takes is a little discipline.

Whenever you have five minutes to spare, whether it's in the early morning, after lunch, or right before bed, make it a habit to spend time alone. Make it nonnegotiable—a necessity as important as eating or sleeping. You won't have days on end to sit, but even a few minutes of intentional, focused sitting will be beneficial for your body and soul. Have a seat.

"YOU'RE MY
PLACE OF
QUIET RETREAT;
I WAIT FOR
YOUR WORD TO
RENEW ME."

—PSALM 119:114 MSG

Sun is good for your health and mood.

Chances are, you've probably heard that your body produces the vitamin D you need when your skin is exposed to sunlight. It helps you feel more awake and more positive, and it is often called the sunshine vitamin.

The sun also helps the foliage and plants you may see near the beach. Wild lilac spreads its intoxicating fragrance. Bearberry pops up on sand dunes and beaches, and animals feed on it during the winter. Wild columbine grows throughout the Great Lakes region. Without the sun, many of these plants would not thrive or even survive.

What can we learn from the sun? We can learn how to nurture ourselves. Just as the sun gives us important vitamins and warms our skin, we need to be sure we're helping our own bodies thrive. In short, we need to take care of ourselves.

Nurturing yourself may look different for you than it looks for your siblings, your parents, or your friends. It can be anything from buying fresh flowers just because they make you happy to making an appointment with a counselor to talk through some worries. You can nurture yourself by taking a long walk one night a week or by making sure to eat plenty of greens. Read the Bible, have coffee with a friend, or ask for help. Make that annual doctor's appointment, take a vacation day, or learn to rewire that negative voice in your head.

For many people, taking care of oneself doesn't come easily. Life is too busy, your personal needs are overshadowed by others' needs, or you simply feel selfish doing it. But just as the sun brings life through its rays, you need to ensure you're taking in rays yourself. When you allow yourself to soak up the sun and all its benefits, you're helping your body, mind, and soul, and your own personal sunshine will radiate into others' lives. Nurture yourself. Soak up the sunshine.

SUNSHINE is the BEST MEDICINE.

LOOK for SEASHELLS.

Found seashells are little treasures.

There are so many kinds—fighting conch, kitten's paw, golden olive, lightning whelk, angel wings, and more. They are scattered along the shore and sitting atop dry sand, and it's fun to explore the beach when you're keeping an eye out for any exceptionally beautiful shells.

Anytime you're searching for shells, especially with children, there are frequent exclamations of "Wow!" or "Look at this one!" Seashell hunting forces you to be mindful of the beauty of creation. And every few minutes you're reminded of the wonder of it all when you pick up another shell, each one different from the last.

Sometimes you have to sift through piles of broken shells or pick up a pile of dirty seaweed to find the most beautiful treasures underneath. Other shells might be so covered in sand that you can't see their perfect forms until you rinse them off. But once you do, you're awed by their simple beauty and intricate designs.

Life is often like seashell hunting. Once your trip to the beach ends and you're back at home, the only nature around may be your houseplants or the tiny patch of grass on your lot. Even so, you can still find ways to gaze at the wonder of creation while living everyday life.

If you have is a park near your home, walk there in the morning as the sun rises and sit on a bench—or even a swing—as you take in the kaleidoscope of colors. You might live in the suburbs, where green lawns are prevalent but breathtaking views are hundreds of miles away. That's okay. Examine the delicate petals of your pansies, run your fingers through the lush green blades of grass, watch the sun reflect rainbows in the streams of the sprinkler.

You may live in the middle of New York City, where skyscrapers line the sky and concrete rules. God's creation is still there. There's more nature than meets the eye—you might just have to search. Walk to a nearby greenhouse or a garden center and take a stroll through the many types of plants. Find the nearest butterfly exhibit and watch the butterflies soar and dip through the air. God's creation is all around if you're willing to look for it.

Discovering the wonders of creation doesn't always mean climbing to a mountain's peak or venturing to the Grand Canyon. Sometimes, after a little digging, you'll find it in the most unexpected places. Just keep your eyes open.

"The earth is the LORD's and the fullness thereof, the world and those who dwell therein, for he has founded it upon the seas and established it upon the rivers."

—Psalm 24:1–2 ESV

"Hurry up!" It's a common phrase

used in our lives today. We hurry to work, hurry to school, hurry through our breakfast and lunch, and we grab dinner on the go. The grocery store has express checkout lines so we can get back on the road at lightning speed. We think the more we can get done by the end of the day, the less stressed we'll feel before closing our eyes at night.

But is it worth it?

We were not created to sprint through every day at breakneck speed or to lie in bed at night with our heads spinning and bodies exhausted. We were not meant to walk around with our shoulders raised to our ears, utterly stressed about all the obligations of today.

Think about your beach days. When you head to the shore, umbrella in hand and smile on your face, what's your main objective? To relax. Unwind. Slow down. You spend long, lingering hours reading, chatting, and simply sitting. You do leisurely things like hunting for shells.

When you search for seashells, your senses come alive. The treasure hunt forces you to slow down. You can't spot gorgeous seashells if you're racing down the beach—they'll be indistinguishable from one another.

It's a simple truth: even if you're flying down the sand

with barely a glance at the shells beneath your feet, they're still there. These tiny gifts of the sea remain, even if you don't see them. And the same is true with your life, isn't it? There are small treasures beneath your feet all day long, but you need to slow down in order to see them. Slow down today.

SLOW DOWN.
HAPPINESS
IS TRYING TO
CATCH YOU.

If you have ever looked for seashells

by the ocean, you know that the best shells aren't always visible—they're often in the water. And in order to walk home with your hands full of unique sea souvenirs, you need to get wet. Sometimes that may feel like a risk.

Getting wet doesn't always seem appealing. Perhaps it's a rainy day, or maybe you aren't dressed appropriately for the water, or maybe the water's a tad chilly. But to find something good, you need to venture in. Sure, there's a big possibility there won't be any shells when you wade in. But then again, there just might be.

This rings true over and over in life, doesn't it? The biggest opportunities may look a little daunting, whether it's introducing yourself to a new friend, applying for a new job, taking that evening class, or trying to patch up a broken relationship.

Maybe you don't feel qualified, the risk seems too big, or perhaps you're just plain shaking-in-your-flip-flops afraid. It's okay to feel those feelings. But what if giving into your fears means you miss what is perhaps the most beautiful shell you've ever seen? You won't find it scanning the edges of the water or walking on dry land.

Getting wet will often feel daunting, but you may emerge with a treasure in the end.

EVERY *seashell*
HAS A *story.*

Beach Rule #5:

BUILD ⚓
SANDCASTLES.

Kids are intent while building sandcastles.

Their eager, creative hands form a masterpiece with just a bucket, shovel, sand, and water. The castles range from simple to extravagant, but no matter the size or stature, children want you to see their creations. They're proud of the work they did with their own hands. Satisfaction shines on their sun-kissed faces.

When is the last time you created something you were proud of? Something you wanted to share or marvel at? Was it something small, like a new cookie recipe, tidy rows in the garden, a new paint color in your bedroom, or a simple piece of pottery? Or was it a huge accomplishment, like your beautiful children, the new company you built from the ground up, or the house you remodeled?

The act of creating something that makes your heart swell with pride often gets buried under stacks of unopened mail. Instead, you need to create with intention. When children go to the beach, they bring their buckets and shovels and sit down in the gritty sand to build a castle.

Grab your proverbial bucket and shovel and make a plan. It's time to begin.

DREAMS ARE
MADE OF
sand AND sun.

Sand is a part of being at the beach.

It gets under your nails and in your bathing suit. It sticks to your face and somehow ends up in your ears. When you get a little sandy at the beach, you probably don't run back to the house to rinse off. Sand is part of the experience.

But something changes when you go home. All of a sudden, grass stains are a big deal. The mud tracked into the entryway gives you a headache. The grime under your nails needs to go. A little dirt is no longer acceptable.

For once, allow yourself to make a mess. Dig in the garden, and relish the feeling of cool dirt in your hands. Let your kids make cookies—and don't rush to their aid when the flour spills all over the counter. Dance in the rain; go camping; eat a melting ice cream cone in the hot sun.

When Jesus healed the blind man by spitting on the ground and making mud from the dust, He didn't walk away with pristine sandals and a starched shirt. When God created the beach and the sea, the birds of the air, and the fish in the ocean, there was most definitely dust and sand involved. But in both of those instances, miracles were happening; a person was healed, and the world was being created. It was messy, but it was also beautiful.

There is a place for cleanliness, but there's also something to be said for getting dirty once in a while. It's just sand, it's just flour, it's just dirt. Don't be afraid to get dirty. It may even be more fun than you anticipated.

No grit, no pearl.

Building a sandcastle is simple.

You need a bucket, a shovel, sand, and water. Anything else is an extravagance. Even if other items might be helpful, they aren't necessary. You can make a tower, a moat, and even add some flair with a few dribbles of wet sand. You can live like a king or a queen in sandcastle world. The castle and the building of it are simple.

Wouldn't it be wonderful if everything in life were as simple as building a sandcastle? Perhaps it could be if we didn't make things so complicated. Maybe instead of using a sand bucket and your hands, you've purchased a sand mold of the Parthenon and a full set of sculpting tools. Maybe you're using a sculpting brush to add some texture when a simple seagull feather or seashells would work just as well.

The quest to live simply isn't as much a lifestyle as it is a choice. Sure, you can choose to fill your schedule with activities and commitments. You can work seventy hours a week and try to get by on as little sleep as possible. Or you can make some changes. Give yourself a budget and a time limit to shop for Christmas presents this year. Clean out your closet—you'll be surprised how less feels like more.

Simple living is a choice. It's not easy, and you won't always succeed—but that's okay. It comes with small choices, day after day. It may not look like selling all your possessions and living in a tiny house for the rest of your life, and it isn't always manageable to walk everywhere instead of driving, especially if the closest grocery store is seven miles away. But you can start somewhere. Take the first step to living simply today.

"It is not how much we have,
but how much we enjoy, that
makes happiness."

—Charles Spurgeon

Beach Rule #6:

RIDE the WAVES.

Riding your first wave can be scary.

Though the waves may seem big and intimidating, there comes a moment when you decide to go for it. You get into the water even though your legs tremble and the water is frigid, you watch for a wave, and then you let it carry you.

The first time might not go well—water might get up your nose or you might be tossed around a bit. But you did it, and that's what matters. But after that first time, riding the waves doesn't seem so scary anymore. You look for a bigger wave, you turn to meet it, and you feel exhilarated. With each swell, you become more confident.

Riding the waves looks a lot like bravery. It looks like being bold. Big or little decisions, settling a conflict, taking a new job, setting boundaries, seeking help, saying no—these are all actions that take some boldness. They take bravery. And they may look insurmountable at times.

You may not always be successful. Life is tricky in many ways, and sometimes even the best intentions or most innocent approach turns into a sticky situation. But more often than not, being bold opens you up to more possibilities, more courage, and a stronger sense of self. You'll gain the respect of others around you, and you'll also respect yourself more.

Take that bold step and ride a wave today.

LIFE ISN'T ABOUT WAITING FOR THE WINDS TO CHANGE ... IT'S LEARNING TO ADJUST YOUR SAILS.

"Have I not commanded you? Be strong and courageous. Do not be afraid; do not be discouraged, for the LORD your God will be with you wherever you go."

—Joshua 1:9

How many times have you stood up

against a wave only to get a torrent of water up your nose? It's inevitable—and uncomfortable too. Fighting the water won't get you very far, but once you let your body drift along with the waves, you will have success—and a dry nose.

God's plan for you may not be what you envisioned. It probably has twists and turns that you didn't expect or want. But you will find one thing to be true: it's better to yield to the waves than to stand resolutely, trying to hold your ground.

You are safe in the hands of your heavenly Father. The One whose voice spoke water into existence and calms the seas has a specific plan just for you. It's a good plan; it's a perfect plan. Rest in that truth today. And the next time a wave appears, sink into its swell and ride it.

There's no better sound than laughter,

and the echoes of it carry along the seashore. Much of the time, laughter comes from children. Children laugh at least three hundred times per day on average, while adults laugh only about fifteen times per day. These statistics may seem startling, but they have been proven over and over again.

Maybe it's different when you're at the beach; maybe you laugh more when you're there. It's easier to laugh when daily stresses are lifted off your shoulders and you're left to bask in the sun and swim in the water. You laugh when trying to ride the waves, a chuckle escapes when a tiny crab emerges from its shell, and laughter fills the air as you fly a kite that competes with seagulls for air space.

It's more difficult to laugh when you're at home, in the dead of winter, after a stressful day at work. Laughter doesn't come easily when your car dies or your bank balance is suffering. You don't dissolve into fits of giggles when your children complain—for the third night in a row—about the dinner you lovingly prepared.

Though there are some areas of everyday life that are simply not enjoyable but must be endured, you can still find ways to live a happier, more laugh-filled life. Try incorporating fun at least once a day. It could mean taking a detour on the way home from work to stop and swing at the park—in business attire and all. Persuade your friends to come over and play a lively game of charades. Plan a weekly coffee date with a friend who can make you laugh, no matter what. Head to the zoo during your lunch break and watch the monkeys perform acrobatics.

Fun looks different for everyone, but laughter always looks the same. Whether you're belly laughing until tears roll down your cheeks or giggling at the silly text your brother sent, it's important to laugh each day, every day, many times throughout.

The next time your day feels a bit dull, ask yourself if you've laughed in the past hour. And if not, try to incorporate a little fun—it's good for your heart, soul, and mind.

The CURE for
ANYTHING is SALTWATER:
SWEAT, TEARS,
or the SEA.

BREATHE in the FRESH AIR.

Breathe deeply. Fresh air invigorates

your senses. As your lungs expand, any sense of stress lifts off your shoulders. As you breathe out, your whole body begins to relax. That's what the simple act of deep breathing can do.

Living life by the water is relaxing for many different reasons, and one reason is the salty air. There's something different about beach air. When you're by the ocean, the tantalizing smell of saltwater can lift your spirit.

Breathing in fresh air does a world of good for your state of mind. It helps untangle a web of to-do lists and worries. It gives your body renewed energy. It invigorates.

Even if you live in a bustling city, you can still "breathe in the fresh air" to a certain extent. You simply need to do what energizes you. Just as fresh air revitalizes you, focusing on things that are life-giving can do the same. What brings life to you? What can cause your cheeks to flush with excitement and lift a load off your back?

For some, baking cookies in the middle of the afternoon offers a reprieve and satisfies a chaotic mind. Others might find enjoyment in going to the farmer's market and holding a juicy tomato warmed by the sun. Maybe it's listening to your favorite music or tackling a house project that requires sweat and power tools.

Find what energizes you, and make it a priority to give your body that breath of fresh air. Doing what you love is an opportunity to feel exhilarated.

"Because he bends
down to listen,
I will pray as long as
I have breath."

—Psalm 116:2 NLT

It's easy to go outside at the beach.

The temperatures are pleasant, the flowers are sunning their faces, and a gentle breeze ruffles tree leaves. Warm, humid air fills your lungs, and it seems almost crazy to stay inside. Why waste beautiful weather?

But when the temperature drops, going outside seems like the last thing you want to do. Even the bare-limbed trees are shaking in the wind, and the comfort of your heated home far outweighs the allure of snow-covered sidewalks.

Even so, it's been said that there is no bad weather, only bad clothing. Think back to your time at the beach when you didn't need any prompting to go outdoors. Remember how alive you felt after a day spent strolling along the shore? Being outside rejuvenates and invigorates, and the same can be true even on the dreariest of days.

You may need layers, a down coat, rain boots, or wool socks. An umbrella, knit hat, or hand warmers might be a necessity. But once you walk out the front door and your blood starts pumping and your lungs fill with fresh air, you'll remember why it is so good to go outside.

"I love to think of nature as an unlimited broadcasting station, through which God speaks to us every hour, if we will only tune in."

—George Washington Carver

Just breathe, you may tell yourself

when your heart rate accelerates. The stresses of your day, the pressures from your job, or the demands of your family can sometimes feel overwhelming.

In times of anxiety, it is helpful to breathe deeply, just like you might do in the mornings at the beach with your coffee in hand and a light blanket on your lap. *Just breathe.*

Breathe in God's peace—the peace that passes all understanding and settles your heart and mind. Remember God's promises to be faithful to you and never to leave or forsake you. Remind yourself of God's loving and gentle presence.

Then breathe out any worries running through your mind. Let go of the argument you had last night. Release the stress about money. Put away thoughts of not being good enough, smart enough, or strong enough. Let God replace your anxiety with His peace.

You can breathe inside or outside, at your desk, in your home, or in your car, for one minute or ten minutes or an hour. You can breathe in God's peace and breathe out your anxiety because God, the Peacemaker and Helper, is near.

"Life with God is not immunity from difficulties, but peace in difficulties."

—C. S. Lewis

Beach Rule #8:

NAP OFTEN.

Is "nap" a foreign concept for you?

Do you wish you had that elusive "time to yourself"?

When you're at the beach, it's easier to nap, rest, and relax. Isn't that what the beach is for, after all? The beach beckons with time to bask in the sun, a chance to read the book that's been gathering dust on your nightstand, and permission to let your mind and body escape from the daily grind. You're able to return home refreshed and sun kissed.

But then regular life closes in. Your obligations aren't bad, but it all seems like so . . . much. You need to cook dinner. It's your turn to bring snacks to soccer practice. You have homework for your grad-school class. The laundry has piled up. Your boss scheduled a 7:00 a.m. meeting for tomorrow, and you need to prep for it. You want to get off the hamster wheel; you want to take a nap; you *need* to rest. But how?

Take heart. Life is busy. It is full of obligations big and small, pressing and routine. It may seem impossible to take time out, to take one day—or even half a day—to step away from running and racing. But you need it. Everyone needs it. When you live life without taking a moment to breathe, you're doing yourself more harm than good.

Live your life in a rhythm of working and resting. Working hard during the week should mean rest and rejuvenation on the weekend. If you simply can't take a full day off, give yourself a few hours or half a day. If you need to, work extra hard during the week so that you're afforded the luxury of filling yourself back up on the weekend.

Try to ensure that rest isn't an unreachable, almost laughable concept in your life. Do something you enjoy—something you're not able to do every day. Ride your bike, hike, grab your journal, light a candle, or watch a movie. Take a nap.

"OUR HEART
IS RESTLESS
UNTIL IT FINDS
REST IN THEE."
—SAINT AUGUSTINE OF HIPPO

In today's world of Pinterest,

Instagram, Facebook, and more, it's easy to look at others' lives with insecurity. Their vacations are more exotic, their homes cleaner, their clothing more fashionable. We wonder, *Does it take more money or more effort?* We push ourselves to work harder and save more, thinking we'll get that luxurious vacation. We scrub and polish our homes, and we stress when the clutter gets out of control. We pull at our clothing, tuck it in, and get it tailored, but then we wonder why it doesn't look the same as the magazine. We try and we strive, and we try and we strive.

It's okay to want a beautiful vacation. Having a clean and inviting house isn't a crime. Looking our best can help our attitude and confidence. But the trouble starts when we strive after these things and they become our only focus. Striving happens in many other areas of our lives too—parenting, being promoted, cushioning the retirement fund just a little more, and so on. Sometimes we just need permission to stop striving.

Think back to your time at the beach. Saltwater was in your hair, the kids were covered in sand, you took a nap in the middle of the day, and your e-mails went unanswered. There was no striving involved—and didn't it feel freeing?

Today, tell yourself, *I give myself permission to stop striving*. It doesn't mean you stop giving your best; it just means you stop trying to *be* the best. That sounds as restful as taking a nap on the beach.

"Cease striving and know that I am God."

—Psalm 46:10 NASB

Naps are considered a sign of laziness

or weakness in our Western culture. People who sleep in are, in our view, not motivated. We compare hours of sleep like Olympian runners—the shortest amount of time wins.

Yet many studies reveal that napping provides great health benefits. It restores alertness, improves mood, and reduces fatigue. Naps can enhance your performance at work, home, or school. Napping improves your memory and your health—even your creativity. Whether you're the CEO of a law firm, an artist, or a sixth-grade teacher, you can benefit from a nap.

If you want to feel happier and be more productive, treat yourself to the mini luxury of a nap. When you wake, you may feel as if you've just returned from a beach vacation. At the very least, you'll feel more rested. What are you waiting for?

Beach Rule #9:

Take LONG WALKS.

In the high-speed, go-go-go nature

of our everyday lives, taking care of ourselves can often fall to the wayside. It gets smothered under other needs—and suddenly we're left feeling worn-out and sick. Our shoulders tense from stress, we've been eating way too much fast food, and we're having constant aches and pains. Does this sound familiar?

Taking care of yourself physically is so important—important enough to do every single day. Remember how much you love taking long walks on the beach? At sunrise, sunset, or anytime in between, long walks on the beach are beneficial for mind and body. How often did you wish you hadn't walked the beach? You probably can't recall a time. Walks on the beach are always a good idea, and they are a great way to take care of your body.

To take care of yourself physically, begin by making small changes in the way you take care of your body, and you'll start to see big results. Add greens to your morning smoothie, make that doctor's appointment you keep putting off, stretch before you go to bed, and drink more water—with a few lemon slices for extra flavor. Sign up for that yoga class, ask a friend to keep you accountable for your eating habits, and introduce a new vegetable to your dinner table every week. And, of course, go for walks. There are countless ways you can take care of yourself.

You only have one body. It's easy to neglect it and even harder to get back on track—we've all been there. It is an uphill climb. But, just like taking walks on the beach, you won't regret it.

"So, whether you eat or drink,
or whatever you do,
do all to the glory of God."

—1 Corinthians 10:31 ESV

A sea cave, a pristine sand dollar,

a tidal pool full of tiny creatures—there's no telling what you might find while walking along the beach. The scenery constantly changes. The tide comes in and goes out, the sand shifts, and waves bring in new treasures. The beach is expansive and begs to be explored from sunup to sundown.

One of the best—and scariest—parts of exploring is the unknown. When you venture off along the seashore, you have no idea what you'll find. Often you're pleasantly surprised. Occasionally you walk home empty-handed, glad for the experience, but ready to be back home. You may even encounter a jellyfish or two. Exploring doesn't mean you'll find a treasure chest every time, but it always holds adventure.

Just as you explore the beach, why not try a little exploring at home? Let your guard down a bit. Explore a new friendship with someone who thinks differently than you. Sign up for that pottery class. It could be your next favorite hobby, or perhaps you'll take home a few lumpy pots, but you'll be better for having tried. If you're debating switching careers, why not update your résumé?

Your exploration may lead you back to where you started, or it may lead you on a grand adventure. Either way, you'll stand a little taller for the courage it took.

Exploration opens up a new world of possibilities. Grab your sandals or your boots, put on some sunscreen or a scarf, and head out the door. Exploration begins with just one step.

"Life is either a daring adventure or nothing."

—Helen Keller

It's been a long day. Your mind races

in a million different directions, and your shoulders are tied up in knots. You know you have a lot to do, but you don't even know where to begin. How can you, when your brain feels like it's in overdrive?

When you feel like that, you have a couple choices: you can let those feelings snowball, leading to a whole lot of stress, or you can go for a walk. Those long walks on the beach don't have to stop when you're surrounded by sidewalks instead of sand, and the physical act of walking will help you more than you know.

Though it's just simple movement, walking is hugely beneficial—especially when you're feeling overwhelmed. Not only does walking help push more blood and oxygen to the brain, it also gives the brain the freedom to wander so you end the walk with a clearer, more rested mind.

Notable people like Steve Jobs, Henry David Thoreau, Beethoven, and many more utilized walking to help boost creativity, clear the mind, and even meet with colleagues. While walking is an easy, everyday mode of transportation, its benefits are important for your productivity and sanity.

If you need to clear your head, put on your walking shoes. Notice how your mind stops racing and your breathing becomes more measured. Feel your muscles loosen as your body warms up; you feel more alive and more able to tackle the work ahead. The worries of the day fall off your shoulders one by one; and as you put one foot in front of the other, your load feels lighter with each step.

"The LORD is my shepherd,
I lack nothing. He makes me
lie down in green pastures, he
leads me beside quiet waters,
he refreshes my soul.
He guides me along the right
paths for his name's sake."

—Psalm 23:1-3

OBSERVE the TIDE.

There is a rhythm the oceans follow.

The waves swell and recede; the tide goes in and out. It affects fishing, sea life, climate, and beachgoers alike. It seems silly to fight against the tide because it's going to continue going in and out even if you try to resist. The best thing you can do is adjust to its coming and going.

The tide has a rhythm, and so does your life. There will be seasons of sorrow and loss, times when the tears won't stop. There will be times when you are filled with joy and hope. You see countless blessings in your life, and they make your heart sing. You may have seasons where you feel alone. You ache for companionship, for someone who understands you. Cry out to God—He hears and He helps.

Just as the trees change in the fall and the sun shines brightly in the summer, you will not stay in the same season forever. If you're in a barren and desolate winter, take heart because spring is coming. If you feel the warm rays of sun in a season of summer, enjoy it. Don't look in dismay at the coming seasons. Bask in the sunlight, and give thanks.

There are seasons of busyness, and then a reprieve comes. Don't be anxious when you feel the seasons changing; they come and they go just as the tide rises and falls. And the One who holds the oceans in His hand and set each star in its place will most certainly be with you through every single season.

"Never give up,
for that is just the
place and time that
the tide will turn."

—Harriet Beecher Stowe

When the tide begins rising, it lifts

everything that was on the sand. An inner tube, a child's sailboat, a plastic shovel. And when the tide gets underneath these things, they're no longer sitting on the sand; they're riding the waves.

Isn't that the way encouragement works? It lifts a person up. The rising tide of encouragement can give others a boost and keep them afloat.

Have you encouraged others lately?

Encouragement comes in many different forms. It can be a long coffee date with a discouraged friend. Encouragement also can look like a card that lists all the ways you're grateful for your mom. It can be the extra-long hug you give your brother when he's frustrated, a hot meal delivered to a tired new mom, or a bouquet of flowers put on your neighbor's doorstep. Encouragement is the simple act of letting other people know that they're seen.

Encouragement is not always the words "good job" or "I'm proud of you." It's also finding opportunities to carry others when their own tide is low. It doesn't only celebrate huge victories; it also celebrates a person just for being. Encouragement gives hope, adds determination, and lifts others' spirits. Just as every boat needs water underneath it to float, every person needs to be lifted up.

A RISING TIDE LIFTS ALL BOATS.

Are you waiting for something?

For a spouse, for a job to come along, for your earnest prayers to be answered? Waiting is hard. It requires patience and hope. Waiting doesn't have a definite end in sight, but you need to have faith that you will, at some point, not need to wait anymore.

As we wait we're dependent on God's timing and faithfulness. It may not be *our* timing, and it might not even be the answer we're looking for, but it is perfect timing—His perfect timing.

The tide, which is orchestrated by the sun and moon and God Himself, comes in and goes out according to His perfect timing every single day. The ocean itself isn't able to change the tide; it is dependent on gravitational pull, just as we are dependent on the Lord.

In the Bible, God told Sarah she was going to have a baby—though she was an old woman at that point, around ninety-one years of age. Yet God's timing was perfect: He gave Sarah a baby named Isaac, and it was through that family line that Jesus was born.

If you're waiting for something, remember that the Lord, who pulls the tide from high to low, knows your need. His timing is always perfect, and He has not forgotten you. May the knowledge of His goodness ease the ache of waiting. And may you fully rely on Him, just as the ocean's tide relies on the sun, moon, and Him.

"The seasons change
and you change,
but your Lord abides
evermore the same, and
the streams of His love
are as deep, as broad
and as full as ever."

—Charles Spurgeon

Beach Rule #11:

READ a
good 🌀🌀
BOOK.

Sitting down with a new book

and a cup of tea is a relaxing escape. Through reading, you can explore the Pacific Northwest, solve a mystery, learn about French culture, and even be transported to your favorite place—the beach. A book jacket with a photo of serene water, a beach umbrella, or pedicured toes gives a big hint: the story probably takes place along the shores of the beach.

For some of us, a beach trip is the only time to read during the year because the rest of our time is so tied up in busy schedules. It's understandable. Sometimes you're so tired, and you just want to relax in front of the television or go to bed early. But you miss some of the great benefits of reading. Besides getting swept away to another time, place, or culture, there are several pluses to being a bookworm.

Reading helps eliminate stress. When you're lost in a story, you're able to forget about your present worries. Getting lost in a book provides a temporary escape to help ease your mind.

Reading also stimulates your brain and expands your vocabulary, meaning you're receiving an education while simultaneously relaxing. It also improves concentration and memory, and heightens empathy. The act of opening a book can even be contagious. If you have children and wish they read more, set the example and grab a book.

With so many benefits of reading, don't limit your reading time to vacations at the beach. Give yourself permission to relax with a good book, and do it often.

"You can never have a cup of tea large enough or a book long enough to suit me."

—C. S. Lewis

You close the book with a contented sigh

and pack up your beach umbrella. It's time to eat dinner, and you've been engrossed in your book for several hours. The sun is beginning to sink, but as you walk back to the beach house, your mind is full.

Though the book's main character is fictional, her struggles speak to you. You feel deep compassion for your own sister who has been battling those same problems for the past few months, and the book gives you even more perspective into the battle. It's one of the greatest benefits of reading: it helps deepen your ability to empathize and feel compassion.

As you read, your mind engages with the story's characters, and you seek to understand them. Reading about other people's emotions shifts your perspective and helps you connect so you understand others' feelings and relate more easily to what they are going through. Your compassion deepens and your heart softens as you read through struggles you weren't familiar with until you understand the pain and burden on a deeper level.

When you arrive home from the beach, challenge yourself to read more. Choose books that explore a person who is different from you. Or read a book about someone in a similar situation as yourself. Not only will your compassion for others grow; you may find that you're able to give yourself more grace, mercy, and kindness.

"Therefore, as God's chosen people, holy and dearly loved, clothe yourselves with compassion, kindness, humility, gentleness and patience. . . . And over all these virtues put on love, which binds them all together in perfect unity."

—Colossians 3:12, 14

The weekend holds countless options.

You could catch a movie with friends, grab dinner at the fancy new restaurant in town, or go and hear some live music. It's fun to get dressed up, go out, and be social—it's a time to wear your high heels, spritz on some perfume, and arrive at home exhausted but invigorated. However, it's nice not to live that way all the time.

Going out with friends and exploring your city, taking a romantic getaway with your spouse, or shopping with your mom or sisters are all good things. But sometimes you need to experience the pleasure of staying in and enjoying time at home.

At the beach, after a day filled with sun and surf, nothing sounds better than a homemade meal with family or friends. You might follow up dinner with card games and s'mores over the kitchen stove. Or perhaps you relish cozying up on the couch and flipping through the pages of the new book you packed. Staying in is part of beach life. You may find a couple of nights to eat dinner in a scenic spot or watch the newest romantic comedy in theaters, but for the most part, life at the beach is full of simple pleasures.

Don't feel bad if you need a few nights in during the week. You weren't created to live life at breakneck speed.

Remind yourself that you're living like you're at the beach—
even if the meteorologist is calling for flurries tomorrow
morning. Then take a long, hot shower, stoke the fire in
the fireplace, make some tea, and enjoy one of life's simple
pleasures: a cozy home.

Beach Rule #12:

LISTEN to the CRASHING WAVES.

The ocean can lull you to sleep.

The *whoosh* sound of the waves breaking on sand is soothing and constant, and the calming effect is instantaneous.

The powerful crashing of waves and the rhythmic sound of water lapping at the shore is a common option for sound machines. It's readily available as iPhone apps in case you need to travel without your white noise machine. The sound of the ocean, even if you live in a landlocked state, often puts people—from infants to adults—to sleep.

For many people, the moment they turn on the machine, their bodies begins to relax. The waves start to crash, and their breathing becomes deeper. Forehead furrows soften, and shoulders relax. It truly is amazing what the sound of the ocean can do.

Similarly, when you get to the beach and hear the distinct sound of the ocean, it's one of the most evocative sounds. The beach experience wouldn't be the same without it. Being at the beach gives you both the opportunity to relax and permission to unwind. It reminds you that your body needs rest, and it soothes your tired mind. The ocean tunes out the rest of the world.

If you're feeling anxious in the night or have trouble

sleeping, pause for a moment before you take a sleep aid. Instead, listen to the waves. You may need to listen to a recording, but your mind will still revel in the soothing sound. Let the waves help lull you into a deep sleep, reminding you of your sweet times on the beach.

Rest peacefully tonight.

THERE'S NO BETTER SOUND
TO HEAR THAN THE OCEAN,
THE WIND, AND
THE RAIN ALL AT ONCE,
LATE AT NIGHT.

Sounds of the ocean can be deafening.

If you're standing on the shore, it's sometimes tough to hear the person beside you. When you're swimming, you might not be able to hear your friend calling your name from her beach towel. Though the ocean can certainly be noisy, it also does something interesting: it blocks out distractions.

The ocean's noise drowns out the rest of the world. When you're swimming underwater, it's just you, your thoughts, and God. Once the distractions are gone, you can only hear the sound of your breathing and the laughter that bubbles up inside of you. It's only when you break through the surface of the water that you hear seagulls crying and children at play.

We all need that time underwater, metaphorically speaking. We need time to block out all distractions and sit with our own thoughts, God's voice, and nothing else.

When we're scrolling through our phone, trying to pour cereal for hungry mouths, or rushing around before work, it is hard to hear that still, small voice. To hear it, we need to quiet our world. We need to walk out into the ocean and say, *Here I am—it's just me.* It's in those quiet, vulnerable times of solitude that your mind and heart can catch up to one another. And it's in those still and intentional moments that God speaks.

Take a few moments in your day to immerse yourself in the crashing waves and block out all distractions.

"Whether you turn to the right or to the left, your ears will hear a voice behind you, saying, 'This is the way; walk in it.'"

—Isaiah 30:21

Do you remember the first time you saw

the ocean, the first time all you could see was water and waves? It probably made you feel small, didn't it? The ocean is a mighty force, and it's good that we remember we are small. We are no match for the ocean and its currents and riptides—it's not our job to battle them.

The ocean reminds us that we are small and we are not God. We don't control the wind and the rain; we can't part the sea or tell the ocean to be still. Nor should we want to. It would be too much for us; we would use that power in selfish ways. That's why it's so good that we have a perfect God who controls all things.

He called the oceans into existence. He poured the sand onto the beach and created every single starfish. Through His creative hand, brightly colored fish came into being, and He formed octopuses and their eight legs. Through His power, God makes it clear that He can handle everything.

However, our culture loves to focus on self. It tells us we need to do everything and be everything. We need to be a loving spouse and an upwardly mobile employee; our homes need to be immaculate and our cars should be shiny. Our society tells us we need to have a platform in order to be heard, and everyone needs a brand to be noticed. It tells us that if we are small, we are not important.

However, God tells us something different. He says we *are* small, and that is okay. In fact, we should take comfort in the fact that we are small. We don't have to have it all figured out, and we don't need to worry about tomorrow.

We have a God who is above all things and who looks at us as His daughters and sons. The ocean reminds us we are small, but our God is the Creator of the heavens, the earth, the sea, and all that is in them (Exodus 20:11). He is all we need.

"RELYING
ON GOD HAS
TO BEGIN
ALL OVER AGAIN
EVERY DAY
AS IF NOTHING
HAD YET BEEN DONE."
—C. S. LEWIS

Beach Rule #13:

DON'T
MISS
the SUNSET.

The sun slowly begins its descent,

dimming its light from bright golden rays into sweet pastel hues. It's sunset time—one of the most anticipated evening moments on the beach, for nothing is more relaxing than seeing the sky turn into an artist's palette. It's restful and quiet, the water gently lapping at your feet, a smile of contentment on your face. You never tire of the sunset at the beach.

However, in the frantic hustle of everyday life, it's easy to miss the sunset, isn't it? Staying inside, you cook dinner, shuffle through stacks of bills, and try to keep your head above water. Stepping outside to watch the sun sink seems almost laughable when your to-do list is ten feet long. But here's the good news: enjoying the sunset, taking time out for yourself, is *not* impossible.

Rest can be incorporated into your everyday life. Yes, it's easier to watch the sunset at the beach; that's a given. But the sun sets every evening, whether you live in a landlocked state, a high-traffic city, or a farm on the plains. All you need to do is make time to see it set.

Take time for yourself tonight. Go outside, even if it's just for five minutes, and listen to the birds performing their night song. Take a deep breath, and let the chaos of the day roll off your shoulders. Close your eyes, and imagine the sound of waves crashing against the shore. Open your eyes, and behold the sunset. God, the Creator of beauty, is also the Creator of rest. He desires for you to quiet your thoughts, heart, and schedule, even on the busiest of days.

So walk outside, open up your heart, and let the worries of the day go.

"I could never stay long enough on the shore; the tang of the untainted, fresh, and free sea air was like a cool, quieting thought."

—Helen Keller

The beach is full of beautiful wonders.

From the multicolored patterns of seashells to the vibrant hues of a beach sunset, there's enough beauty to make your breath catch in your throat.

Yet we forget about the beauty of God's small gifts to us in our ordinary, everyday lives. We choose to focus on the frustrating events of the day. When we sit down to watch the sunset at the beach, however, we're choosing to reflect on the beauty surrounding us. The cares and distractions of the world may still be there, but we aren't focusing on them during sunset.

Can you do that today? Keep your eyes open for beauty, for things large and small that make your heart sing. It may be the smell of chocolate chip cookies baking in the oven or the sound of your children giggling. Focus on beauty, and don't be distracted. Beauty is everywhere.

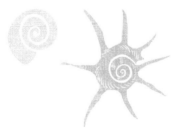

"How many are your works,
LORD! In wisdom you
made them all; the earth
is full of your creatures.
There is the sea, vast and
spacious, teeming with
creatures beyond number—
living things both large
and small."

—Psalm 104:24-25

Why does a beach day feel so restful?

The answer is simple: priorities are different. Priorities are less about getting work finished and more about rest and relaxation. Power suits are replaced by swimsuits, hair is blown dry by the salty sea air, and the only e-mail sent is an out-of-office reply. At the beach, there is less *doing* and more *being*. "Don't miss the sunset" becomes the only agenda item.

Then you go back home. Bills, packing lunches, and meeting agendas replace leisurely evenings of watching the sunset. Your mind becomes harried, your fuse gets shorter—life becomes more complicated. But it doesn't need to be that way.

In the early-morning hours, instead of scrolling through e-mails and Instagram while sipping your requisite cup of coffee, make it a priority to get your mind and heart ready for the day. Pray, stretch, and take note of the tiny blessings scattered throughout your house.

During the afternoon, when you're tempted to snap at a colleague who has made a big mistake, make it a priority to speak kindly, love generously, and give grace freely.

When evening comes and you're feeling harried and neither you nor your spouse has any idea of what to make for dinner, make it a priority instead to nourish your relationship.

Call for takeout, order a pizza, or pick up soup from the neighborhood deli. A shift in priorities can do a whole lot of good for your mental well-being, can't it?

And finally, be sure to occasionally forego the usual evening rituals, bundle up the kids, and watch the sunset on the lawn. Cuddle close as you ooh and ahh over the changing colors—you're making memories.

"Peace is seeing the sunset and knowing whom to thank."

—Unknown

Beach Rule #14:

LEAVE your TROUBLES BEHIND.

When you take a beach vacation,

you leave your troubles behind. You don't check your work e-mail, responsibilities are delegated, and you're free to relax. What a delight! You can connect with your family, play Frisbee with friends, jog next to the shore, and completely disconnect.

At the beach, you leave your troubles behind without a second thought.

Once you're back at work, however, you know that freedom is over. You need to clock the hours—forty, fifty, or even seventy hours a week—at the office. You sleep little and work a lot. Your family gets used to eating dinner without you, and your spouse often goes to bed alone. But is it necessary?

Be encouraged: you can live like you're at the beach. It will take discipline and will go against any workaholic instinct, but it can be done. Studies have shown that productivity

declines significantly when the workweek exceeds fifty hours—and after fifty-five hours, productivity does not increase at all. Did you read that correctly? Anyone working more than fifty-five hours (sixty, seventy-five, even eighty) is really only completing fifty-five hours of work.

The ability to work is a gift—a privilege from God. But too often we tend to abuse this gift and turn it into something less like a gift and more like a burden. If you're living life for work—and only work—something has to change.

It's less about the amount of work you put in and more about balance—work/life balance. When you're constantly working with no chance to rest, it's only a matter of time before you burn out. Your work suffers, your relationships suffer, and you become an exhausted and weary mess. Your carefree days at the beach seem like a dream.

Yet people who recharge and reconnect on the weekend are much more successful than those who use the weekend for work. Weekends set up your week for better or for worse. If you disconnect from work, pursue some of your passions, spend quality time with family and friends, and carve out time for yourself, you'll go into the workweek much more rested and focused. Your mind has the chance to relax, your body has time to rest, and you come to work Monday morning with excitement rather than dread.

What would it look like to live your weekends as though you were at the beach? Why don't you try working a little less? Relax, recharge, and reconnect. Use the weekend as a weekend, and leave work for the workweek.

"It is senseless for you to work so hard from early morning until late at night, fearing you will starve to death; for God wants his loved ones to get their proper rest."

—Psalm 127:2 TLB

"Out of the abundance of the heart

the mouth speaks," Jesus said in Matthew 12:34 (ESV). This is startling, but it is also true. Think about what happens when you hold anger in your heart. You probably grumble under your breath, snap at your spouse, or rant to a coworker. Because your heart is angry, your mouth speaks angry words.

When you feel joyful—if you've just had a baby, if you finally feel the sun after a long, cold winter, or if you've received a promotion at work—your words are happy. You speak with excitement and wonder, you smile and laugh, and your mouth reflects the way your heart is feeling.

Your beach days are filled, more often than not, with happy times. Who can be angry when the sunset is more beautiful than the finest art? No one can resist a laugh when jumping in the waves. The stress of everyday life lifts off your shoulders at the beach, and your thoughts and conversations are more positive. You're a pleasure to be around, and you aren't beating yourself up at the end of the day for all the words you wish you hadn't said.

It's painless to think and speak positively when life feels easy. When it feels hard, it's a whole different story. It takes practice. It takes practice to compliment others or to quiet that voice of self-doubt in your mind. You'll find yourself biting your tongue more than once, and you will probably slip up many times. But the more you practice, the better you'll get.

Make a list of things you're grateful for, and read it every morning. As you begin thinking and speaking more positively, your heart and mind will begin to change. Others will see a difference in you. Your joyful attitude and your practice of leaving your troubles behind are bound to be contagious. Begin filtering your thoughts and guarding your tongue, and your heart will be abundantly filled with joy.

"No pessimist ever discovered
the secrets of the stars, or
sailed to an uncharted land,
or opened a new heaven to
the human spirit."

—Helen Keller

Beach Rule #15:

MAKE ⚓
MEMORIES.

Some of life's best memories are made

at the beach: the boat rides and the waterskiing, the smell of saltwater in your hair, those early-morning walks when the beach is still quiet. So many memories remain vivid, even after the last load of laundry is washed and summer settles into fall.

That one summer you turned red as a lobster after trying to bronze your skin quickly—you can laugh about it now. Your first experience of summer love and awe-inspiring thunderstorms stay tucked in your memory. You remember all the nights you sat with the family declaring that this sunset was the summer's best, only to repeat the same thing the next night . . . and the next. You can practically hear your dad's booming laughter after your first attempt at waterskiing, and the scent of honeysuckle always reminds you of the path leading to the beach house.

Living and experiencing every moment created lasting memories at the beach. You heard, saw, smelled, tasted, and touched different things every day, and they all combined to form some of your life's best memories.

You may not be able to live at the beach 365 days a year. Your home may be in the rolling hills of Pennsylvania or the cornfields of Wisconsin. You might live in the city amidst

skyscrapers and
office buildings or in
the suburbs of west
Michigan. Wherever
your home lies, even
if it's not by the beach,
you can still make
equally heartwarming
memories.

Live your life as you would at
the beach. Put down your phone and
unplug from social media, even for a couple hours. Create
space in the day to walk through your neighborhood and
marvel at your neighbor's garden. Take pictures in your mind
instead of with your phone, and be social with your friends
instead of being hooked on social media. Savor the last bites
of dinner instead of racing to get the kids off to bed. See
your life. Listen to your life. *Live* your life. And make lots of
memories.

"I came so that they could have life—indeed, so that they could live life to the fullest."

—John 10:10 CEB

More, more, more. Our culture values

accumulating things, and it often feels normal to go along with that mind-set. We want the newest iPhone model; we buy new curtains because ours feel a bit dated; we shop till we drop and then some more, but we never really feel satisfied.

Why? *More* isn't the answer. Of course, a new dress may make us feel happy for a few days, or a new car will feel luxurious for a while, but at the heart of it, stuff doesn't matter. Experiences do.

Chances are, your experiences are more meaningful to you than anything you've owned over the years. You can probably recall the first time you rode a jet ski and the exhilaration you felt during the ride or the taste of the strawberry shortcake your grandmother made after a day in the water. You fondly remember holding your parents' or grandparents' hands as you jumped wave after wave.

You recall the days of skimping and saving so your family could have a week at the beach, and you don't miss any of the "stuff" you didn't buy. Memories at the beach will last a lifetime; stuff lasts only for a little while.

If you want to make memories that you'll look back on fondly for years to come, focus more on experiences and less on material possessions.

Do you like to know what's ahead?

Do you need to have your days scheduled? Is a tidy to-do list part of your morning routine? The world needs planners— men and women who measure their courses of action and carefully weigh their options. But a scheduled life can sometimes feel a little stagnant, and it can also feel very busy with a rigid timeline and no option of veering off course.

Have you thought about making room for spontaneity? Think about your time at the beach. When the sun is out, you're on the beach, searching for shells, flying kites, watching the sunset in your favorite spot. But often there's a rainy day or two, and suddenly your plan of lying on the beach and working on your tan isn't feasible.

Rainy days require some creativity and a bit of spontaneity. On those rainy days, you pull out the board games, make a fort in the living room, and hop in the car for ice cream, dodging raindrops as you come back. Spontaneity isn't always convenient, but it can be rewarding.

Even when you're back in your regular routine, you can incorporate some of your beach life into your everyday life. Instead of the usual spaghetti on Wednesday night, try a new recipe or order a restaurant entrée you've never tried before. Make a little time in your morning schedule to surprise your spouse with breakfast in bed. On your lunch break, take a detour and walk through the city's museum. Loosen your fist from your schedule every once in a while—spontaneity is good for the soul.

And on rainy days, it's always a good idea to get some ice cream.

THE OCEAN is CALLING
and I MUST GO.